ALL AROUND TOWN

CONTENTS

4x5 DOOR

1x2x3 WALL ELEMENT

1x1x2 HINGE BRICK AND WINDOW SHUTTER

1x6 TILE

2x4 PLATE

2x2 TILE

2x2 TILE

2x3 PLATE

HOME ESSENTIALS
Door and window pieces are useful for building houses. Mix and match colors and styles if you don't have enough of one!

1x6 ARCHED FENCE

1x2x2 WINDOW FRAME

6x6 TILE

BUSH

2x3 CURVED PLATE WITH HOLE

FLOWER

FLOWER

DO IT YOURSELF!
If you haven't got a ready-made piece, try to recreate it yourself.

BALL JOINT

LUGGAGE CART

USE REAL BUILDINGS AS INSPIRATION. THEN ADD SOME IMAGINATION!

1x1 CORNER PANEL

FLOWER WITH OPEN STUD

SMALL TREE

BARRED WINDOW WITH 2 CONNECTIONS

CARROT

CHERRIES

BAMBOO PLANT

FLOWERS AND STEM

LARGE PLANT LEAVES

FAUCET

USE WHAT YOU HAVE
Be innovative with your bricks. If you don't have a ladder, turn this barred window (above) on its side! (See Children's Bedroom, p.9)

(See Children's Bedroom, p.9)

1x2 PLATE WITH SIDE RAIL

1x2 TEXTURED BRICK

CRATE

THE GREAT OUTDOORS
Remember to build both indoor and outdoor spaces to make your scene as realistic as possible.

TELESCOPE

1x4x1 LATTICE FENCE

1x4x2 LATTICE GATE

1x4x2 BARRED FENCE

1x8 PLATE WITH SIDE RAIL

ORNAMENTAL ARCH

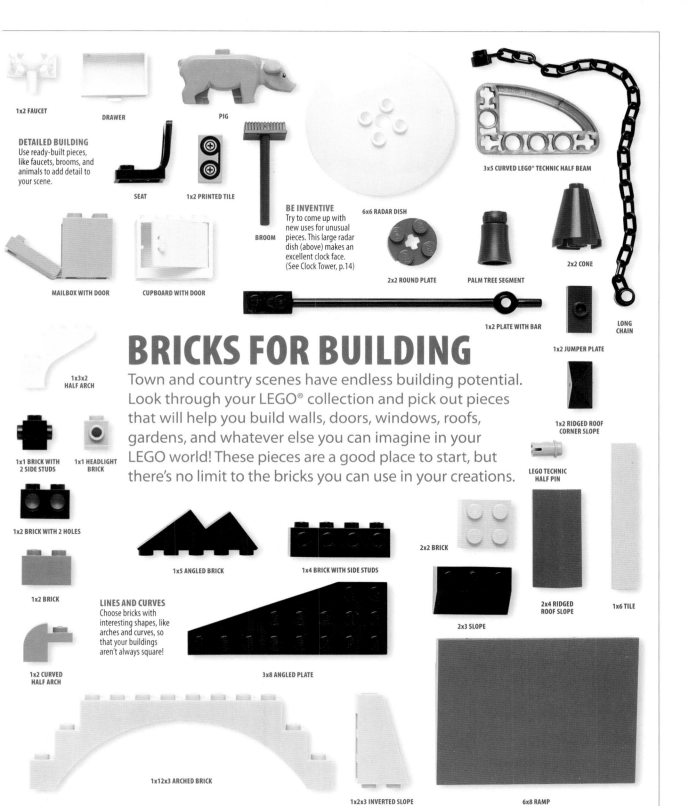

1x2 FAUCET

DRAWER

PIG

DETAILED BUILDING
Use ready-built pieces, like faucets, brooms, and animals to add detail to your scene.

SEAT

1x2 PRINTED TILE

BROOM

BE INVENTIVE
Try to come up with new uses for unusual pieces. This large radar dish (above) makes an excellent clock face. (See Clock Tower, p.14)

6x6 RADAR DISH

2x2 ROUND PLATE

PALM TREE SEGMENT

3x5 CURVED LEGO® TECHNIC HALF BEAM

2x2 CONE

1x2 PLATE WITH BAR

LONG CHAIN

1x2 JUMPER PLATE

MAILBOX WITH DOOR

CUPBOARD WITH DOOR

1x3x2 HALF ARCH

BRICKS FOR BUILDING

Town and country scenes have endless building potential. Look through your LEGO® collection and pick out pieces that will help you build walls, doors, windows, roofs, gardens, and whatever else you can imagine in your LEGO world! These pieces are a good place to start, but there's no limit to the bricks you can use in your creations.

1x1 BRICK WITH 2 SIDE STUDS

1x1 HEADLIGHT BRICK

1x2 BRICK WITH 2 HOLES

1x2 BRICK

1x2 CURVED HALF ARCH

LINES AND CURVES
Choose bricks with interesting shapes, like arches and curves, so that your buildings aren't always square!

1x5 ANGLED BRICK

1x4 BRICK WITH SIDE STUDS

2x2 BRICK

3x8 ANGLED PLATE

2x3 SLOPE

1x2 RIDGED ROOF CORNER SLOPE

LEGO TECHNIC HALF PIN

2x4 RIDGED ROOF SLOPE

1x6 TILE

1x12x3 ARCHED BRICK

1x2x3 INVERTED SLOPE

6x8 RAMP

FAMILY HOUSE

Town construction is all about making detailed models of real buildings—and what could be better than making a home for an entire LEGO family? Plan out your bricks before you start, to see which colors you have the most of. Do you want matching doors and windows? Two floors or three? This is your house—the design is up to you!

BUILDING BRIEF
Objective: Build big family houses
Use: Sleeping, cooking, living, dining
Features: Must be strong and sturdy, removable roof
Extras: Furniture, satellite dish, front and back yards

If you don't have enough roof pieces and slopes, use plates and hinges to build an opening roof!

You could make each floor a different color

HOUSE BUILDING

Start your house with a basic brick outline, and decide where you want to put the doors and windows before you make the walls. Plan the layouts of your rooms as you build so everybody has enough space—and remember, you'll want to add furniture, so leave space for that, too!

SURE, I'LL REBUILD THE HOUSE THIS WEEKEND!

YOU'LL HAVE TO ASK YOUR FATHER, DEAR.

CAN'T I HAVE A BIGGER ROOM? PLEEEAAASE?

Garden—use flowers, trees, and colorful 1x1 plates to design your outdoor space

There are many different types of doors and windows. Will you stick to one style for your family house—or mix and match?

Real lawns aren't totally flat, so use a few plates to add depth

You could build a bigger yard, and add sheds, swings, or even a swimming pool!

EASY ACCESS
Make each floor removable by lining the tops of the walls with tiles. Use just a few plates with exposed studs to hold the next level in place.

Inner walls built into outer walls for strength to support upper levels

EXPLODED VIEW

Choose where to place your staircase before finalizing the room layout

Each row of roof tiles is supported by a layer of bricks underneath

Each floor is about seven or eight bricks high

Textured bricks add detail and decoration

Balcony railing made from barred fence

BRICKS IN THE WALL
If you don't have enough of one color, build walls with stripes or other patterns. You could try to replicate the look of real bricks —or use crazy colors!

Front walkway, built with tiles. You could add a welcome mat, too!

GROUND FLOOR

What does a minifigure family need? Take a look at real houses to decide what rooms and furniture you want. The ground floors of most houses have a foyer, dining room, and kitchen, but maybe you want to build a playroom or den as well?

Bookshelf. The sides are made from curved LEGO Technic half beams

Table lamp, built from just two pieces

Curved pieces make furniture look soft

LIVING ROOM

Stretch out the middle of a comfy chair and you've got a family couch!

Shiny wood floor, made with tiles. You could add a rug, using colored pieces, or a thick carpet, using studs

DINING ROOM

Cabinet drawers with handles, made from jumper plates

Make extra tile tablecloths for special occasions

Table legs made from telescopes

KITCHEN

THIS PLACE HAS EVERYTHING PLUS THE KITCHEN SINK!

Stove, built from a mailbox and two printed videotape tiles

FURNITURE

When building furniture, look at your pieces in new ways. Turn them around or upside-down and see if you can discover part of a chair, lamp, or sofa. Remember to build your furniture to minifigure scale!

STAIRS

The stairs in this house use a long rubber piece for the handrail, supported by skeleton legs. If you don't have these pieces, you could use 1x1 bricks in alternating colors and 1x1 slopes.

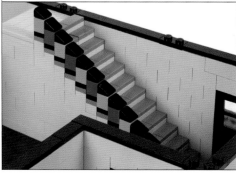

TOP FLOOR

Every member of the family is an individual, so all the bedrooms in the house should be distinct, too. Make each one show the interests and personality of whoever sleeps there. You could also put in a guest room, storage room, or games room!

BATHROOM

If you don't have these faucet pieces, try to build your own!

Use 1x1 tiles for a patterned floor

Could you add an opening lid?

Bathtub sides made from curved half arches built in opposite directions

TOP FLOOR FURNITURE

When you're building the same piece of furniture a few times, try to make each item unique. Experiment with sizes, colors, and styles, and think about how a child's furniture is different from an adult's!

LAMPS

Modern floor lamp made with two radar dishes and an antenna

Master bedroom doors open out onto balcony

Long tiles create wooden plank effect

Crystal lamp base made with transparent plates

For stability, build the balcony directly into the floor of the top story

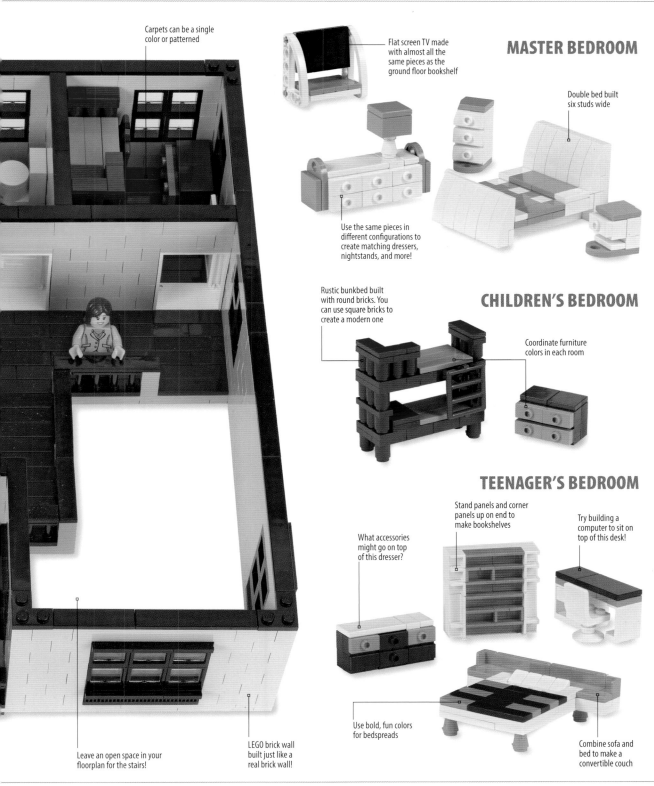

Carpets can be a single color or patterned

Flat screen TV made with almost all the same pieces as the ground floor bookshelf

MASTER BEDROOM

Double bed built six studs wide

Use the same pieces in different configurations to create matching dressers, nightstands, and more!

Rustic bunkbed built with round bricks. You can use square bricks to create a modern one

CHILDREN'S BEDROOM

Coordinate furniture colors in each room

TEENAGER'S BEDROOM

Stand panels and corner panels up on end to make bookshelves

Try building a computer to sit on top of this desk!

What accessories might go on top of this dresser?

Use bold, fun colors for bedspreads

Combine sofa and bed to make a convertible couch

Leave an open space in your floorplan for the stairs!

LEGO brick wall built just like a real brick wall!

MICROBUILDINGS

Want to build a whole town or city, but don't have much space? Try creating microbuildings! With just a handful of standard bricks, a few special pieces here and there, and lots of imagination, you can build a landscape that is tiny, but hugely impressive!

LIGHT AND COLOR
Use transparent plates to create the look of stained-glass windows. You may not be able to capture the intricate detail of the real thing, but the idea will shine through!

BUILDING BRIEF
Objective: Create microbuildings
Use: Part of a microscale town or city
Features: Lots of detail at a tiny scale
Extras: Tiny people, cars, neighborhoods

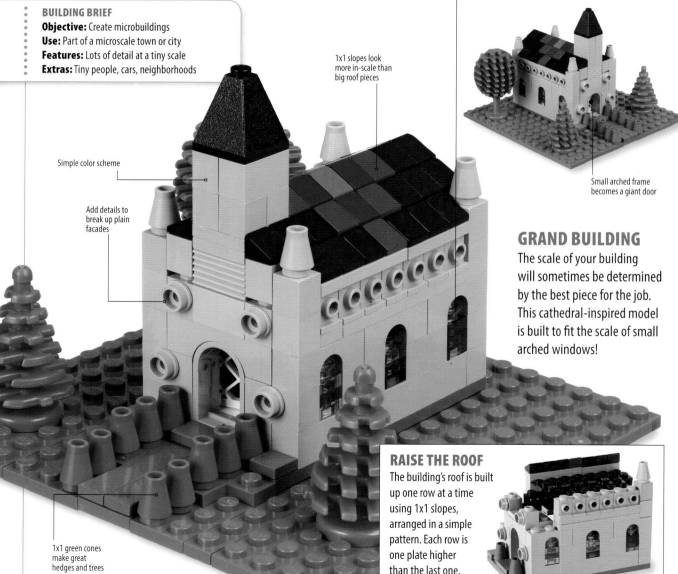

Simple color scheme

Add details to break up plain facades

1x1 slopes look more in-scale than big roof pieces

1x1 green cones make great hedges and trees

Small arched frame becomes a giant door

GRAND BUILDING
The scale of your building will sometimes be determined by the best piece for the job. This cathedral-inspired model is built to fit the scale of small arched windows!

RAISE THE ROOF
The building's roof is built up one row at a time using 1x1 slopes, arranged in a simple pattern. Each row is one plate higher than the last one.

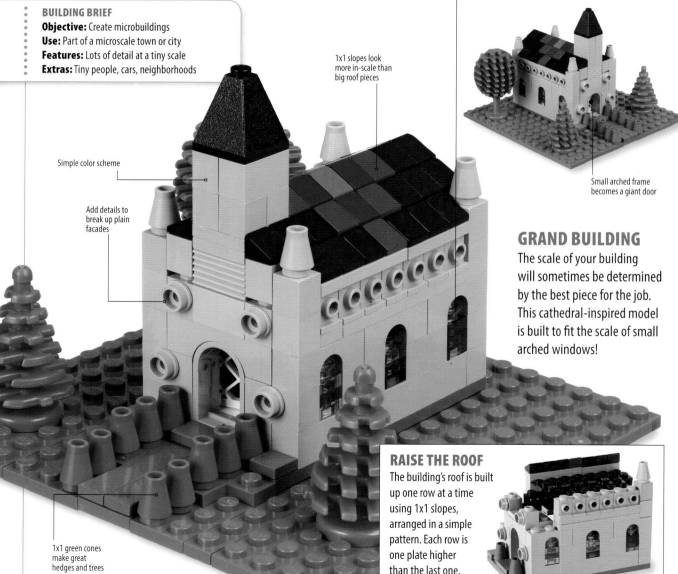

Building fronts don't have to be angular—try using curved slopes

Textured bricks add detail

CANAL HOUSE

Photographs can help you design locations from a particular time or place, like this Dutch canal house. Keep the proportions as close as possible to the real thing.

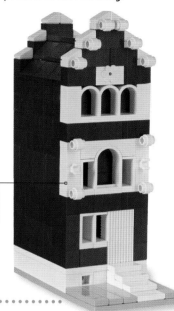

STREET STORES

For a row of buildings, start with a street base, made of plates and tiles. Create each building separately and then attach it to the base. Give each one its own distinct lines, like the green and orange store's curved roof.

Try to choose interesting color combinations

Add awnings and overhangs to entrances

Building and trim have contrasting colors

Add simple decorative details, but don't overdo it

REAR VIEW

MICROHOUSE

Don't just build a boring box for your microscale house. Experiment with different shapes and pieces! Pick out your windows and doors first so you know how big to make the rest of the building around them.

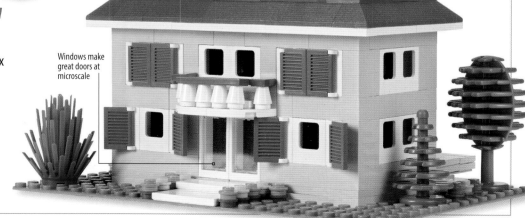

Same roof pieces as on big houses—just fewer of them!

Windows make great doors at microscale

TRAIN STATION

A train station is a functional building, but that doesn't mean it has to look boring! Try to design your station in an unusual shape, and give it some interesting features, like arched doorways, striking brickwork, or a unique roof. You could even build a removable roof so you can access the interior for rebuilding and play.

BUILDING BRIEF
Objective: Build train stations
Use: A place for passengers to get tickets and wait for their trains
Features: Ticket desk, indoor and outdoor waiting areas
Extras: Trains, signal lights, signs, train tracks

Roof built in an elongated hexagonal shape

GETTING INTO SHAPE
Building a roof in an unusual shape can be tricky, so focus on this aspect of the model first. When the roof is complete, build the walls to fit.

I'M LATE! DO LEGO TRAINS RUN ON TIME?

ARCHES
Two half arches form the top of a fancy doorway, while a single half arch piece can be used to support part of the roof.

Elevate the main building on a platform to draw attention to it

ROOF REVEALED

It takes lots of experimentation to get the sides of the roof's angled plate sections to line up just right without leaving any big gaps.

Experiment with angled plates until you get the shape you want!

Roof attaches to just a few studs for easy removal

Different color patterns resemble real brick walls

STATION MASTERING

If you don't have a lot of room inside your building, pick the most important features to include. Do you want ticket desks, benches, shops, or locker rooms?

FLOWER POWER

Happy vegetation really brightens up a public building. You can use plates, tiles, and panels to make flower boxes to decorate your station!

STATION BUILDINGS

It takes more than one building to make a train station!
Look at real stations to get ideas about what else your
scene could include. Each building should be different from
the others, but perhaps you could incorporate common
elements into each of them so they all fit together.

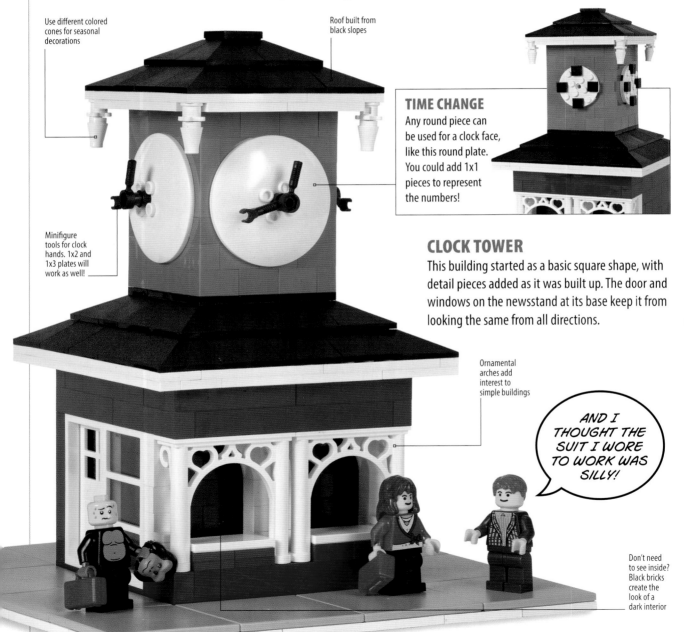

Use different colored
cones for seasonal
decorations

Roof built from
black slopes

TIME CHANGE

Any round piece can
be used for a clock face,
like this round plate.
You could add 1x1
pieces to represent
the numbers!

Minifigure
tools for clock
hands. 1x2 and
1x3 plates will
work as well!

CLOCK TOWER

This building started as a basic square shape, with
detail pieces added as it was built up. The door and
windows on the newsstand at its base keep it from
looking the same from all directions.

Ornamental
arches add
interest to
simple buildings

*AND I
THOUGHT THE
SUIT I WORE
TO WORK WAS
SILLY!*

Don't need
to see inside?
Black bricks
create the
look of a
dark interior

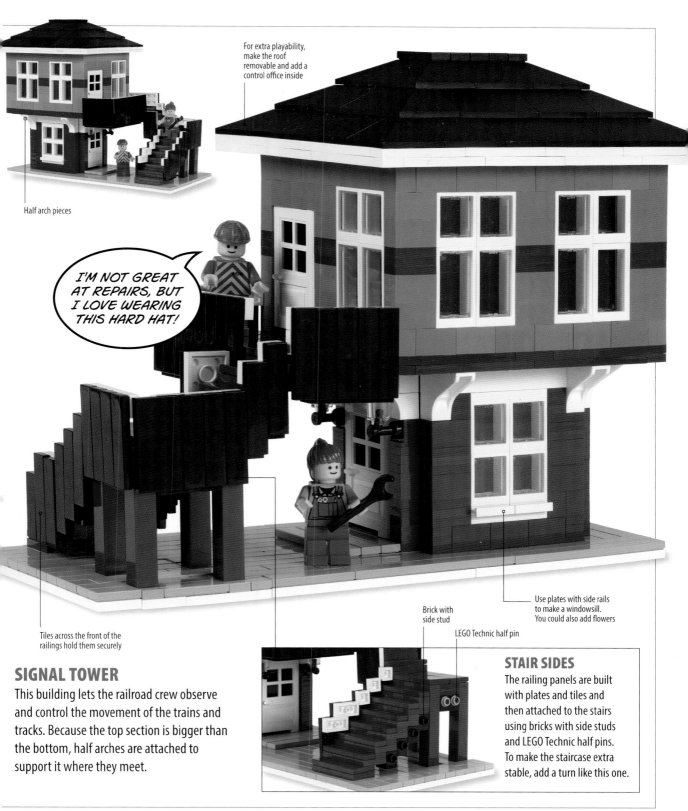

For extra playability, make the roof removable and add a control office inside

Half arch pieces

I'M NOT GREAT AT REPAIRS, BUT I LOVE WEARING THIS HARD HAT!

Use plates with side rails to make a windowsill. You could also add flowers

Brick with side stud

LEGO Technic half pin

Tiles across the front of the railings hold them securely

SIGNAL TOWER

This building lets the railroad crew observe and control the movement of the trains and tracks. Because the top section is bigger than the bottom, half arches are attached to support it where they meet.

STAIR SIDES

The railing panels are built with plates and tiles and then attached to the stairs using bricks with side studs and LEGO Technic half pins. To make the staircase extra stable, add a turn like this one.

INSIDE THE STATION

There are lots of great things you can build inside your train station, from rows of seats and departures desks, to check-in counters and x-ray scanning machines. You could also build waiting rooms, machines, and ticket counters for a bus station—or even an airport. Now all you need to do is get your minifigures ready to travel!

DEPARTURES

This is the departure gate, where passengers hand over their tickets before boarding the train. The simple desk is made from red and white pieces, with no sideways building.

You could use transparent pieces to cover the studs and act as desk lights

BUT I CAN'T SIT NEXT TO HER— WE'RE WEARING THE SAME TORSO!

This ticket counter could also be an airport check-in desk!

TICKET COUNTER

White bricks with tiles on top make this ticket counter look sleek and hi-tech. Computer screens are positioned at an angle on jumper plates, and the keyboards are attached with a clip and bar hinge so they can be positioned at an angle.

You could build the computer desks in the colors of your railway company

Same-color minifigure torsos look like uniforms

SORRY, BUT MY THREE INVISIBLE FRIENDS ARE SITTING HERE.

SITTING AROUND

Build your waiting area for as many passengers as you like. These red seats clip onto a 2x12 plate. The feet are 1x2 jumper plates with 1x1 round plates on top. Don't forget to add a small side table. Remember: it's all about the details!

2x2 tile used as tabletop

Jumper plates evenly spaced out

X-ray machine—gray tiles, small panels, and cones make it look functional

SECURITY ALERT!

Security is an important feature in airports and some train and bus stations. Make sure your x-ray machine is the right size to scan LEGO luggage, and that the body scanner is tall enough for a minifigure—and his hat—to walk through!

Keyboards and computer screens can be found in various LEGO® City sets, but you could use a plain tile or a grille instead

X-ray scanner, made from specialized angled pieces. A stack of 1x2 bricks with slopes on the top corners would work just as well

COUNTRY BARN

Want a break from the hustle and bustle of the big city? Head out to the countryside and build yourself a farm, starting with a good old-fashioned barn. Make it big and sturdy, with plenty of room for animals, crops, and equipment inside. Farming life is hard work, but building it can be lots of fun!

BUILDING BRIEF
Objective: Build barns for your farms
Use: Storage of food, tools, and livestock
Features: Opening doors, lots of space
Extras: Farming equipment, granary, farm animals

BARN RAISING

The roof is the trickiest part of this model, so build it first, leaving a narrow groove in the underside so it can slot securely onto the barn walls and be removed easily. Match the trim around the doors and windows to the colors of the roof.

Weather vane—try different animals on top, too!

Vary shape and size of windows

Use 1x3 slopes for the upper roof and 1x2 slopes for the lower roof to get a perfect barn shape!

Don't have enough slopes for roof tiles? Use plates instead!

With winch parts, you could make the hayloft crane really work

AHHH...DON'T YOU JUST LOVE THAT FRESH COUNTRY AIR?

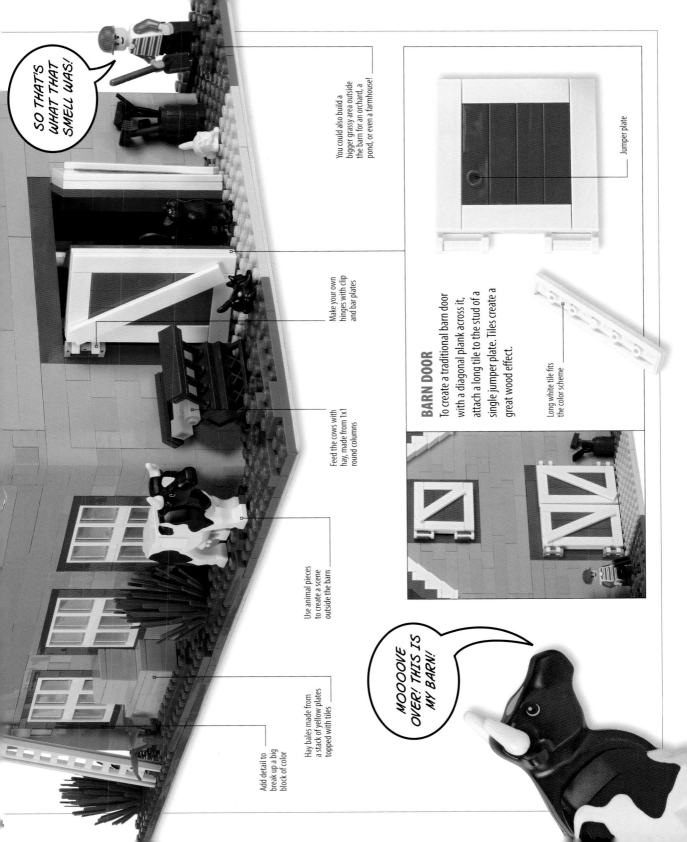

SO THAT'S WHAT THAT SMELL WAS!

You could also build a bigger grassy area outside the barn for an orchard, a pond, or even a farmhouse!

Jumper plate

BARN DOOR

To create a traditional barn door with a diagonal plank across it, attach a long tile to the stud of a single jumper plate. Tiles create a great wood effect.

Long white tile fits the color scheme

Make your own hinges with clip and bar plates

Feed the cows with hay, made from 1x1 round columns

Use animal pieces to create a scene outside the barn

Hay bales made from a stack of yellow plates topped with tiles

Add detail to break up a big block of color

MOOOOVE OVER! THIS IS MY BARN!!

FARMYARD LIFE

With the right bricks and pieces, you can create a whole farm for those hard-working minifigures. Think about what kind of farm you want to run—a dairy farm, an orchard, a ranch—and bring it to life!

BUILDING BRIEF
Objective: Build whole farms
Use: Milking, sowing, feeding, harvesting
Features: Coops, pens, orchards, natural surroundings
Extras: Tractor, field, stable, pen, farmer's house

Some duck houses are built on an island in the middle of a pond. Where will yours go?

COOL COVER

The angled roof of this duck house is made from large ramp pieces, which are built up and locked together with basic plates. You could even attach the roof with a clip and bar hinge so you can play inside!

HOLD ON? THIS IS NICER THAN MY HOUSE!

BRICK FOWL

If you don't have the right LEGO animal, make your own! This duck is made using a few simple colors and pieces, like clip-plate wings and a bill made from a 1x1 cone.

DUCK HOUSE

A duck house doesn't have to be a plain, white hut! Design an unusual roof, add lattice windows, or build it on a raised platform so the ducks can wander underneath.

DUCK POND

A pond isn't clean and smooth like a swimming pool, so build yours to look wild and untamed, with plants and mud around the edges.

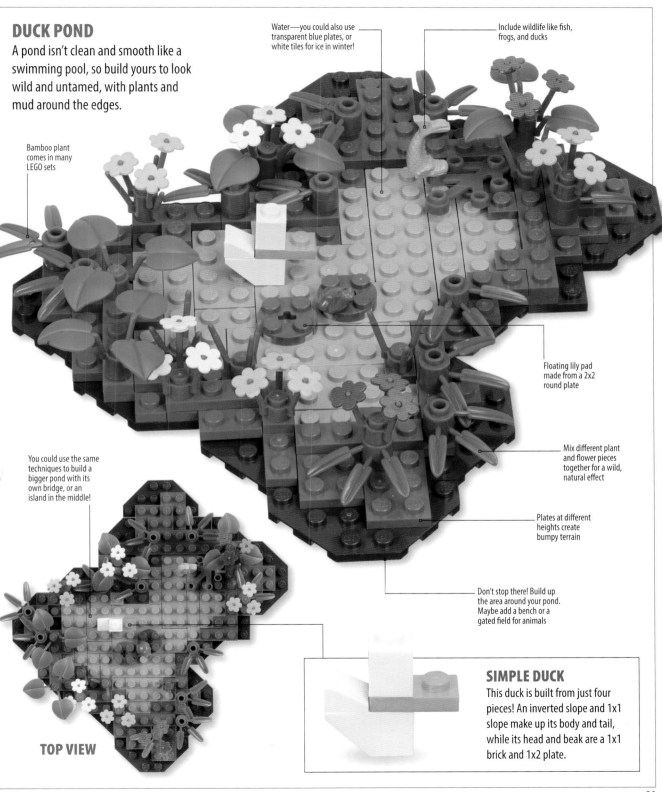

Water—you could also use transparent blue plates, or white tiles for ice in winter!

Include wildlife like fish, frogs, and ducks

Bamboo plant comes in many LEGO sets

Floating lily pad made from a 2x2 round plate

Mix different plant and flower pieces together for a wild, natural effect

Plates at different heights create bumpy terrain

You could use the same techniques to build a bigger pond with its own bridge, or an island in the middle!

Don't stop there! Build up the area around your pond. Maybe add a bench or a gated field for animals

TOP VIEW

SIMPLE DUCK

This duck is built from just four pieces! An inverted slope and 1x1 slope make up its body and tail, while its head and beak are a 1x1 brick and 1x2 plate.

DOWN ON THE FARM

To bring your farm creations to life, think about the small details: What does a shed's roof really look like? How can you build a realistic gate? What fruit will be growing in your orchard? Don't stop until you're really happy with your model!

TIN ROOF

Long, gray plates with side-rails look like a sheet of corrugated metal when attached side-by-side.

Roof is attached to shed with a 1x6 jumper plate

A plate hung diagonally adds decoration

THAT'S A WHOLE LOTTA FARM TO WATER. I'LL NEED A BIGGER CAN.

TOOL SHED

To make your doors (or windows) look smaller than they are, build a doorway the size you want, then place the door behind it so it opens inward.

DON'T HOG ALL THE FOOD, HAMLET!

A clean, square fence on rough, uneven terrain makes a good visual contrast

PIGPEN

You don't want farm animals to run wild and eat your crops, so build some enclosures! Instead of a single-piece base, this sty has layers of plates to give its surface some depth.

Mud doesn't stay inside boundaries, so let it flow out past the fence

Gate made from lattice gate attached upside-down

BRICK FRUIT
If you don't have pieces of LEGO fruit, make your own! Round or square red bricks make great apples, or use yellow for lemons. Can you think of any other pieces to use?

You could add flowers to your trees, too!

Palm tree segments come in many LEGO sets—or you could use round bricks

Build a strong, wide base to support a tall tree

ORCHARD
You could build a well-tended orchard with rows of straight, matching trees—but your farm will look more natural if your tree trunks and branches are different shapes.

If it's fall, your tree may have fewer leaves on it

Why not build a whole vegetable patch with rows of lettuces, carrots, and tomatoes?

Carrot growing out of the ground is really a 1x1 brick topped with a 2x2 plate!

2x2 round plate

EASY AS ONE, TWO, TREE
Building your own trees is easy! Stack round brown bricks or plates on a sturdy base for the trunk, then add plant leaves or any green pieces as leaves.

Use green plates if you want your tree to have a base of grass

BRIDGES

It's easy to snap some plates together and call it a bridge, but if you really want to cross a gap with style, try making a bridge that looks like the real thing—and works like it, too. Here's a great way to build a gentle humpback bridge for a park or country river crossing.

BUILDING BRIEF
Objective: Build bridges
Use: Crossing streams, rivers, and ditches
Features: Strength, stability, walls, railings
Extras: Cars, pedestrians, tollgates, nighttime lights

HUMPBACK BRIDGE

To build this picturesque bridge, start with a central arch. Make a solid base around the arch shape, building steps into it to create height. Then use slopes and tiles to create a smooth finish.

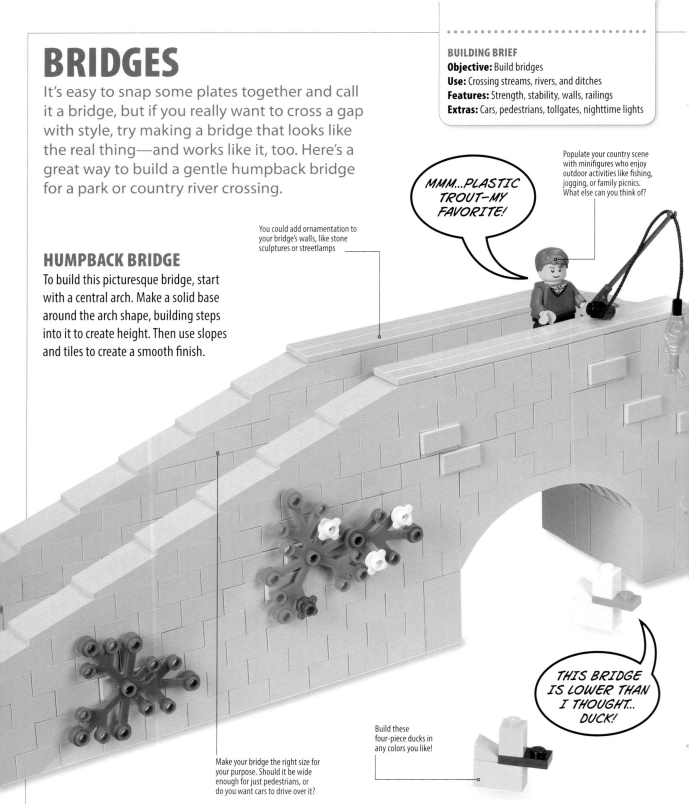

You could add ornamentation to your bridge's walls, like stone sculptures or streetlamps

Populate your country scene with minifigures who enjoy outdoor activities like fishing, jogging, or family picnics. What else can you think of?

MMM...PLASTIC TROUT—MY FAVORITE!

THIS BRIDGE IS LOWER THAN I THOUGHT... DUCK!

Make your bridge the right size for your purpose. Should it be wide enough for just pedestrians, or do you want cars to drive over it?

Build these four-piece ducks in any colors you like!

MINI ARCH

The arch is built just like the ones on the big model, but with fewer bricks. Use smaller arch pieces for even tinier bridges.

Arched brick

MICROBRIDGE

You can build a bridge in microscale, too! Try to include all the key features of a bigger model, like arches, support columns, railings, and a smooth pathway across.

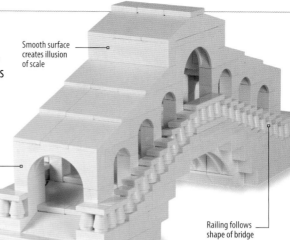

Smooth surface creates illusion of scale

All-white bricks look like polished marble

Railing follows shape of bridge

Use slopes to make the walls follow a gentle curve. You could also use plates to build gradual steps

You could also make a base for your bridge to sit on. Build it up with grass, trees flowers, and a river

Attach plant leaves and flowers to jumper plates built into the bridge walls

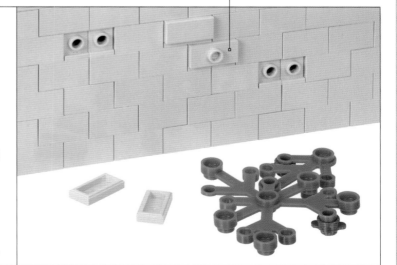

Your bridge doesn't have to be built out of tan bricks. Use brown pieces for a rustic wooden bridge, or gray for old stone

BULGING BRICKS

To make some of the stones bulge out from your wall, include headlight bricks among your 1x2 bricks and attach 1x2 tiles to them.

BIGGER BRIDGES

For larger spans of water, you need a bigger bridge! Large bridges usually have more arches to support their length and weight. They're made out of the strongest materials around, so use lots of gray bricks to mimic stone, or LEGO Technic pieces for metal girders.

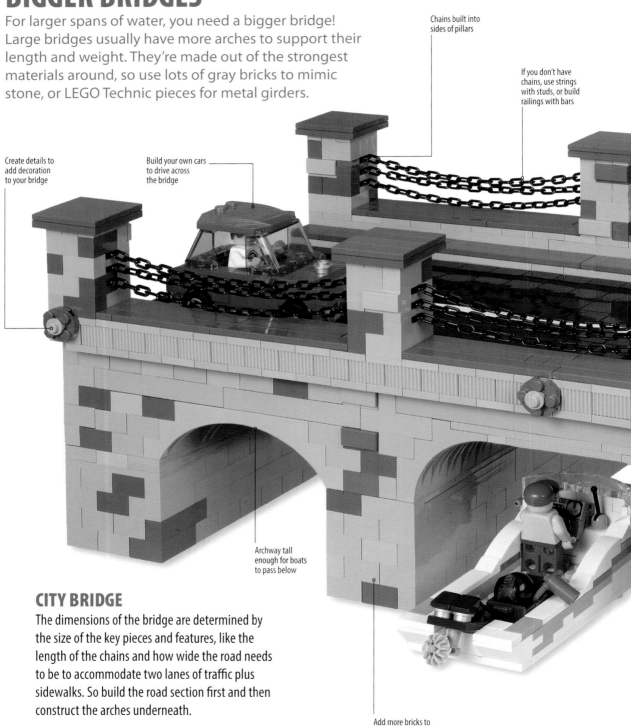

Chains built into sides of pillars

If you don't have chains, use strings with studs, or build railings with bars

Create details to add decoration to your bridge

Build your own cars to drive across the bridge

Archway tall enough for boats to pass below

Add more bricks to make supports taller!

CITY BRIDGE

The dimensions of the bridge are determined by the size of the key pieces and features, like the length of the chains and how wide the road needs to be to accommodate two lanes of traffic plus sidewalks. So build the road section first and then construct the arches underneath.

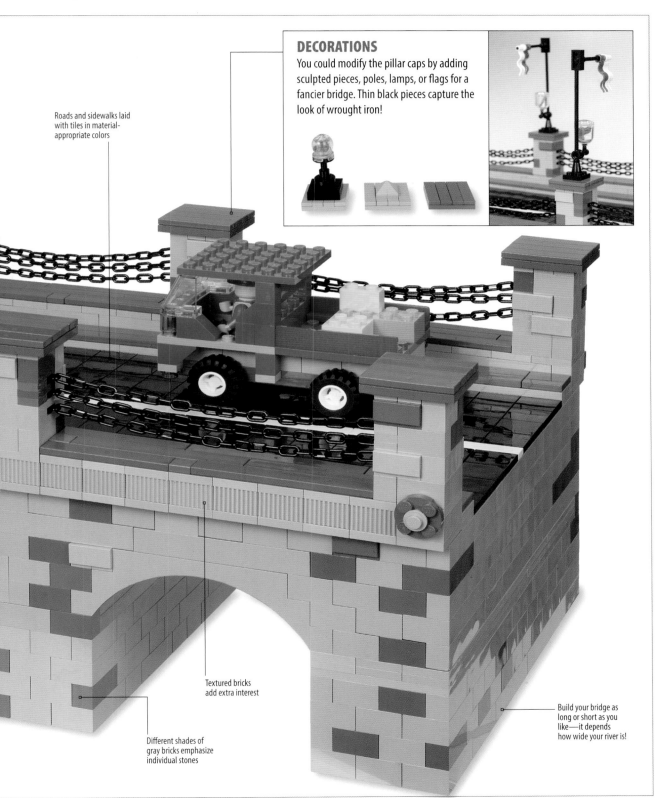

Roads and sidewalks laid
with tiles in material-
appropriate colors

DECORATIONS

You could modify the pillar caps by adding
sculpted pieces, poles, lamps, or flags for a
fancier bridge. Thin black pieces capture the
look of wrought iron!

Textured bricks
add extra interest

Different shades of
gray bricks emphasize
individual stones

Build your bridge as
long or short as you
like—it depends
how wide your river is!

DK | Penguin Random House

Editor Shari Last
Additional Editors Jo Casey, Hannah Dolan, Emma Grange,
Matt Jones, Catherine Saunders, Lisa Stock, Victoria Taylor
Senior Editor Laura Gilbert
Designer Owen Bennett
Additional Designers Lynne Moulding, Robert Perry,
Lisa Sodeau, Ron Stobbart, Rhys Thomas, Toby Truphet
Jacket Designer David McDonald
Senior Designer Nathan Martin
Senior DTP Designer Kavita Varma
Producer Lloyd Robertson
Managing Editor Simon Hugo
Design Manager Guy Harvey
Creative Manager Sarah Harland
Art Director Lisa Lanzarini
Publisher Julie Ferris
Publishing Director Simon Beecroft

Photography by Gary Ombler,
Brian Poulsen, and Tim Trøjborg

Acknowledgments
Dorling Kindersley would like to thank: Stephanie Lawrence, Randi Sørensen, and
Corinna van Delden at the LEGO Group; Sebastiaan Arts, Tim Goddard, Deborah
Higdon, Barney Main, Duncan Titmarsh (www.bright-bricks.com), and Andrew
Walker for their amazing models; Jeff van Winden for additional building; Daniel
Lipkowitz for his fantastic text; Gary Ombler, Brian Poulsen, and Tim Trøjborg for
their brilliant photography; Rachel Peng and Bo Wei at IM Studios;
and Sarah Harland for editorial assistance.

First published in the United States in 2015 by DK Publishing
345 Hudson Street, New York, New York 10014

Contains material previously published in
The LEGO® Ideas Book (2011)

001—284611—Mar/15

Page design copyright © 2015 Dorling Kindersley Limited.
A Penguin Random House Company.

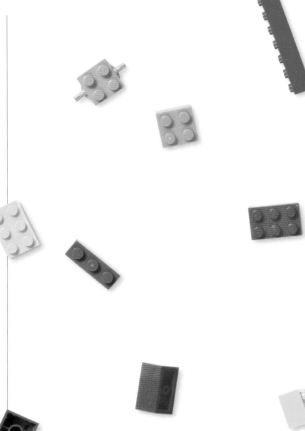

A catalog record for this book is available from the Library of Congress.

ISBN: 978-5-0010-1303-7

Printed in China.

www.dk.com
www.LEGO.com

A WORLD OF IDEAS:
SEE ALL THERE IS TO KNOW